Alsatian Cuisine

Évelyne SEVRIN

Dormonval

CH – LUCERNE

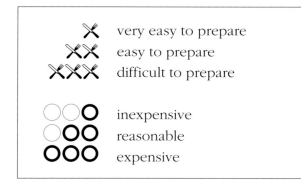

✗	very easy to prepare
✗✗	easy to prepare
✗✗✗	difficult to prepare
○○●	inexpensive
○●●	reasonable
●●●	expensive

Photographs: SAEP/Jean-Luc SYREN, Valérie WALTER and Alain THIÉBAUT.

Drawing: Benoît ROTH.

The translation and english adaptation by EURHODE Traduction.

The dishes were prepared by SAEP/Jean-François CAMPAGNE.

Coordination: SAEP.

Composition and photoengraving: SAEP/Arts Graphiques.

Printing: European Union.

Conception: SAEP CRÉATION
68040 INGERSHEIM - COLMAR

« $\mathcal{A}$ beautiful garden »

This was how Louis XIV described Alsace. Indeed, a much sought-after garden... which is understandable. A very original region, extending over barely 200 km from Wissembourg to the Alsatian Jura. The only thing missing in the garden is a view of the sea.

Although Alsace is, without a doubt, the most coherent French region, it is a land of contrasts, not only between north and south, but even more so between east and west. Its vineyard, the pride of its people, extends harmoniously between the fertile plain and the steep slopes of the Vosges.

But Alsace is, above all, its people, with their straightforward character mixed with the neighbouring Swiss and German mentalities. Alsatians may be a little chauvinistic (but less so than some of their neighbours) and fight to preserve their identity. This is still reflected in the many flower-decked villages and attractive little towns, but no longer the same in the three largest cities, Strasbourg, Colmar and Mulhouse.

However, even there, in spite of all the many influences which are difficult to contain, the charm of the traditional districts attracts growing numbers of delighted visitors. But at Christmas and during the long summer, the way to an Alsatian's heart is via his cuisine, which is both grandiose and available to all.

J.C. B.

Riewele soup

150 g flour / 2 eggs / nutmeg / 1.5 l of beef stock / Salt, pepper.

○○○○● ✕   Prep: 10 min   Serves 6
                            Cooking: 15 min

    Mix the eggs and flour in a bowl. Season with salt and pepper and add the nutmeg. Work the dough to produce «riewele» (small pieces of dough about 5 mm thick).

Heat the stock.

Poach the riewele in the stock for 10 minutes.

Serve very hot.

Lentil soup

250 g lentils / white part of 1 leek / 3 carrots / 1 onion / 1 potato / 100 g smoked bacon / 1 bay leaf / 40 g of butter / 40 g of flour / 2 pairs of Strasbourg sausages / Salt, pepper.

○○●● ✕   Prep: 15 min – Cooking: 2 h   Serves 6
                            Soaking time: 1 h

    Wash the lentils in abundant water. Leave them to soak for 1 hour.

    Boil 3 l of water. Pour in the drained lentils. Add the white of leek, carrots, onion and the potato chopped into cubes.

    Chop the smoked bacon into cubes and add it to the soup along with the bay leaf. Season with salt and pepper. Leave to simmer for 2 hours on a gentle heat.

    Brown the butter and flour and add it to the soup to thicken it.

    Add the sliced sausages towards the end of the cooking time.

Onion soup with melted cheese

30 g butter / 3 large onions / 30 g flour / 1.5 l of stock / 4 slices of white bread / 100 g of grated cheese.

Serves 6   Prep: 10 min
          Cooking: 20 min

✗ ⬤ ◯◯◯◯

Heat the butter in a saucepan. Brown the sliced onion rings. Add the flour before they turn brown.

Add the stock and heat for 15 minutes.

Pour the soup into pottery soup bowls.

Butter the slices of bread lightly.

Top each bowl with a slice of bread.

Sprinkle with grated cheese and put under the grill for 5 minutes.

Serve immediately.

Alsatian asparagus

4 kg asparagus / 30 g coarse salt.
For the mousseline sauce: *20 cl thin fresh cream / 2 egg yolks / 100 g butter / Salt, pepper.*
For the mayonnaise: *1 egg yolk / 1 teaspoon mustard / 10 cl oil / Salt.*
For the French dressing: *2 tablespoons vinegar / 4 tablespoons oil / 1 onion / 1 clove of garlic / Salt, pepper.*

○○●● ✗✗   Prep: 20 min   Serves 8
            Cooking: 30 min

Peel and wash the asparagus. Cook the stalks in boiling salt water for 30 minutes. Drain them and arrange them on an asparagus plate so that they can drain fully. Serve with the 3 sauces: mousseline, mayonnaise and French dressing.

To prepare the mousseline sauce: pour the cream, egg yolks and butter into a salad bowl. Season with salt and pepper. Put the bowl over a water-bath and heat gently while beating the mixture until a foamy sauce is formed.

Mix the egg yolk and mustard for the mayonnaise. Add the salt. Pour in the oil slowly while beating with a balloon whisk.

For the French dressing, mix the oil and vinegar. Season with salt and pepper. Add the chopped onion and garlic.

Dandelion salad

500 g dandelion leaves / 150 g smoked bacon cubes / 1 onion / 10 cl oil / 10 cl vinegar / Salt, pepper.

 Prep: 5 min
Cooking: 5 min

Serves 4

Wash the dandelion leaves well.

Brown the smoked bacon cubes and chopped onion in the oil and add the vinegar.

Arrange the still hot bacon on the salad.

Season with salt and pepper.

Potato salad

1 kg potatoes / 25 cl stock / 1 onion / 3 pickled gherkins / 100 g bacon cubes / Parsley / Salt, pepper.

 Prep: 10 min
Cooking: 25 min

Serves 4

Boil the washed potatoes in boiling water for 20-25 minutes.

Peel them while they are still hot. Cut into slices and put into a salad bowl. Pour in the hot stock. Salt and pepper to taste.

Add the sliced onion and gherkins.

Fry the bacon cubes and add them to the salad with the chopped parsley.

Mix carefully to avoid breaking up the potato.

Serve luke-warm.

Alsatian salad

6 cervelat sausages / 600 g hard cheese / 3 tomatoes / 3 hard-boiled eggs / 1 onion.
French dressing: *2 tablespoons vinegar / 4 tablespoons oil / Chopped parsley / Salt, pepper.*

Serves 6   Prep: 10 min

Remove the skin from the cervelat. Cut the sausages in two lengthways.

Cut crosses into the sausage on the rounded side. Set them out in the centre of a plate.

Add grated cheese around them.

Decorate the plate with tomatoes and hard-boiled eggs chopped into quarters. Sprinkle with sliced onion rings.

Season with the French dressing.

Foie gras

1 fresh foie gras weighing 500 g / 8 g salt / 2 g pepper / 2 g sugar / 4 cl Gewurtztraminer / 2 strips of bacon.

○**OOO** ✘✘✘ Prep: 1 h – Cooking: 45 min   Serves 6 to 8 ○
Marinate: 12 h

Remove the gall and nerves from the liver, cutting into the lobes.

Season with salt and pepper and sugar which have been previously mixed together. Knead the liver with your fingers. Place it in a dish.

Pour the Gewurtztraminer over it while mixing.

Cover the container and leave to marinate in a cool place for 10 hours.

Line a dish with bacon strips. Put the liver in, pressing it down to fill the dish evenly. Cover with bacon strips and put the lid on.

Bake in the oven at 120° C (gas 4) in a water-bath for 45 minutes.

Leave to cool for 2 hours before serving or put it in the fridge, pressing it with a slab and 500 g weight.

Remove excess solid fat for another use. Clean the edges of the dish. Serve the foie gras in slices or with a spoon.

Smooth cottage cheese/quark with fresh cream

1 kg of 40% fat smooth cottage cheese / 125 g fresh cream / 2 onions / 4 cloves of garlic / Chives / Salt, pepper.

◯◯◯◯ O ✗   Prep: 10 min   Serves 6 ◯

Mix the cottage cheese with the fresh cream. Season with salt and pepper.

Chop the onions and garlic finely. Cut up the chives. Put onions, garlic and chives in 3 different bowls. Season the cheese to taste.

Serve with smoked potatoes (p. 42) or baked potatoes.
You can also spread it on country bread or walnut bread.

Savoury Kougelhopf

25 g brewer's yeast / 30 cl milk / 500 g flour / 2 eggs / 200 g butter / 150 g smoked bacon cubes / 20 g salt.

◯◯◯ OO ✗✗✗   Prep: 1 h – Cooking: 45 min   Serves 8 ◯
Proving time: 2 h

Mix the yeast with 15 cl of heated milk.

Mix the flour, eggs and salt in a bowl.

Gradually add the remaining 15 cl milk. Add the softened butter and the yeast-milk mixture.

Mix vigorously, beating the dough for 20 minutes, lifting it with your hand and beating it against the walls of the bowl. The dough must not cling to your hands when it is ready.

Cover the bowl and leave the dough to prove for 1 hour, in a warm place.

Cut the bacon into small cubes. Mix them into the dough, kneading gently. Put the dough into a buttered kougelhopf mould.

Leave to prove again in a warm place.

It should be just above the edge of the mould.

Bake at 150° C (gas 5) for 45 minutes.

Filled Cervelat

6 cervelat sausages / 6 slices of hard cheese / 2 tomatoes /
1 onion / Parsley / 6 slices of smoked bacon.

○○**OO** ✗
Prep: 10 min
Cooking: 15 min

Serves 6 ○

Chop the cervelat sausages lengthways, without com-
pletely separating the two halves.

Fill the interior of each cervelat with a slice of cheese,
several slices of tomato, chopped onion and parsley.

Close the sausages and hold the edges together with a
slice of smoked bacon wrapped around it and held in
place with a toothpick.

Place the filled cervelats in an oven dish and heat in a
hot oven at 200° C (gas 6-7) for 15 minutes.

Put the dish under the grill for 1 minute just before
serving.

Stuffed potatoes

6 large potatoes / 300 g minced beef / 100 g sausage meat /
1 onion / 2 cloves of garlic / 100 g grated cheese / 20 g but-
ter / Salt, pepper, parsley and chives.

OO ✗✗
Prep: 20 min
Cooking: 30 min

Serves 6 ○

Peel the potatoes. Chop them lengthways.

Mix the minced beef, sausage meat, onion and garlic in
a bowl. Season with salt and pepper. Add the chopped
parsley and chives.

Hollow out the potato halves and stuff them with the
meat mixture. Sprinkle with grated cheese. Butter an oven
dish and arrange the potato halves in it.

Bake in a hot oven at 200° C (gas 6-7) for 30 minutes.

Alsatian snails

4 dozen snails / 25 cl vinegar / 20 g coarse salt / 50 cl Sylvaner / 1 onion / 2 shallots / 1 carrot / Parsley / 1 bay leaf / Thyme.
For the butter: *250 g butter / Parsley / 2 shallots / 6 cloves of garlic / Salt, pepper.*

○○○○ ✗✗   Prep: 30 min – Cooking: 3 h 20 min   Serves 4
            Soaking time: 2 h

Soak the snails in vinegar and coarse salt for 2 hours.

Wash them several times in abundant water. Plunge them into boiling water for 5 minutes. Remove the snails from their shells and remove any traces of mucous.

Put them in a saucepan with 50 cl water and the Sylvaner. Add the chopped onion and shallots, the carrot chopped into thin slices, the parsley, bay leaf and thyme. Season with salt and pepper. Leave to simmer gently for 3 hours. Put them in a dish to cool.

Mix the softened butter and finely chopped parsley, shallots and garlic.

Put a little cooking water into each shell with one drained snail. Fill the hole with previously prepared butter.

Place the snails in a snail dish and bake in a hot oven at 220° C (gas 7-8) for 15 minutes.

Breaded Munster cheese

*100 g breadcrumbs / 50 g crushed hazelnuts / 2 egg yolks /
4 small Munster cheeses / 50 g flour / 2 teaspoons cumin /
40 g butter.*

Prep: 10 min
Cooking: 10 min

Serves 4

Mix the breadcrumbs and hazelnuts. Bind the mixture
with the egg yolk. Roll the cheeses in the flour. Coat them
with the breadcrumb-hazelnut-egg mixture. Sprinkle with
cumin. Place a knob of butter on each cheese.

Put them on an oven tray. Bake in a hot oven at 220° C
(gas 7-8) for 10 minutes.

Put them under the grill for 1 minute before serving.

*Note: breaded Munsters go very well with sautéed potatoes or a simple
green salad.*

Gnocchi

*10 raw potatoes / 5 cooked potatoes / 125 g flour / 1 egg /
25 cl fresh cream / 1 onion / Parsley / Salt, pepper.*

Prep: 30 min – Cooking: 10 min
Resting time: 10 min

Serves 6

Peel the raw and cooked potatoes.

Grate the raw potatoes with a cheese grater. Wrap them
in a clean tea-towel for 10 minutes. Press them to squeeze
out the juice.

Put the cooked potatoes through a mixer.

Mix cooked and raw potatoes with the flour, egg, fresh
cream and chopped onion. Season with salt and pepper.

Use two spoons to form the dough into 6 cm long oval
shapes. Plunge them into boiling salted water and leave to
cook for 6 to 7 minutes.

Drain the gnocchi and arrange in a dish. Sprinkle with
chopped parsley.

«Tartes flambées» (Alsatian onion-bacon-cream tart)

500 g bread dough / 1 kg thick fresh cream / 500 g bacon cubes / 5 onions / Salt, pepper.

○○○○**O** ✗

Prep: 15 min
Cooking: 5 to 15 min

For 5 tarts ○

Split the dough into five. Roll each piece out into a rectangle.

On each rectangle, spread 200 g cream with a ladle. Sprinkle with bacon cubes and sliced onion rings. Season with salt and pepper.

Bake in a bread oven for 5 minutes.

If you don't have a bread oven, bake in a very hot oven at 260° C (gas 8-9) for 15 minutes.

Serve immediately.

Note: Today there are many variants on tarte flambée; you can add grated cheese, mushrooms, munster cheese, snails… according to taste.
It is usual to bake one tart after another so that they are eaten really hot.

Onion tart

5 cl oil / 1 kg large onions / 30 g flour / 3 cl fresh cream / 100 g grated cheese / 3 eggs / 500 g shortcrust pastry dough / Salt, pepper.

OO ✗✗

Prep: 10 min
Cooking: 40 min

Serves 8 ○

Heat the oil in a frying pan and cook the chopped onions. Turn them frequently and don't let them brown.

Add the flour while continuing to mix. Pour in the fresh cream. Season with salt and pepper.

Off the heat, stir in the grated cheese and eggs.

Line a shallow dish with the pastry and pour in the mixture when it has slightly cooled. Bake in a hot oven at 220° C (gas 7-8) for 25 minutes.

Serve immediately.

Valley Pie

100 g butter / 2 onions / 500 g chopped pork / 500 g minced beef / 2 eggs + 1 egg yolk / 25 cl fresh cream / Parsley / Chives / 500 g flaky pastry / Salt, pepper.

○○**OO** ✗✗

Prep: 15 min
Cooking: 1 h

Serves 8

Cook the chopped onions in the butter. Mix them with the chopped pork and beef. Add the whole eggs and the cream. Season with salt and pepper.

Chop the parsley and chives finely and fold them into the mixture.

Butter a pie dish. Line it with half the pastry, so that the excess hangs over the edge. Fill it with the mixture. Raise the pastry all round and cover with the other half of the pastry. Weld the edges together with your fingers and brush with egg yolk.

Bake in a hot oven at 220° C (gas 7-8) for 1 hour.

Serve with a green salad.

Fried carp

*1 large carp / 15 cl oil / 2 lemons / 125 g flour / 4 eggs / 100 g
breadcrumbs / Salt, pepper.*

Prep: 20 min – Cooking: 10 min   Serves 6
Marinate: 1 h

Scale and gut the carp. Cut out the fillets in small slices.
Marinate them in the oil and lemon juice for 1 hour.

Wipe them with kitchen paper. Dip them in the flour
then in the salted, beaten eggs and then in breadcrumbs.
Fry them in a fish-fryer for 8 minutes. Drain them. Fry
them a second time for 2 minutes after dipping them into
the egg again.

Serve very hot with boiled potatoes.

Sauerkraut with fish

*500 g pike / 500 g perch / 500 g carp / 1 kg sauerkraut /
1 clove of garlic / 1 onion / 100 g goose fat / 1 bay leaf /
5 juniper berries / 25 cl Alsatian white wine / 25 cl stock /
50 g butter / 1 teaspoon of cognac / Salt, pepper.*

Prep: 30 min   Serves 6
Cooking: 2 h 30 min

Scale, gut and clean the fish. Wash and drain them and
cut them into portions. Keep them in a cool place.

Wash the sauerkraut in cold water. Drain.

Brown the chopped garlic and onion in the goose fat in
a deep saucepan with a thick base. Add the sauerkraut.
Add the bay leaf and juniper berries. Season with salt and
pepper. Fill to mid-height with the wine and stock. Leave
to simmer gently for 2 hours, stirring from time to time.

Brown the fish pieces in butter in a frying pan. Add
them to the sauerkraut and leave to cook for another
30 minutes, adding a little water.

Before serving, add the rest of the butter, heated until it
turns to a warm brown, and the cognac.

Trout with almonds

6 trout / 60 g flour / 200 g butter / 1 tablespoon oil / 100 g flaked almonds / Salt, pepper.

 Prep: 30 min
Cooking: 15 min

Serves 6

Wash, gut and clean the trout. Season with salt and pepper and roll them in the flour.

Melt half the butter in the hot oil.

When the mixture is spitting, lay the trout into the frying pan.

When the skin is golden, lower the heat and leave to cook for 5 minutes on each side. Arrange them on a plate.

Add the other half of the butter to the pan with the flaked almonds. Cook for a few minutes more.

Pour over the trout. Serve immediately.

Trout Meunière

4 trout / 60 g flour / 2 shallots / 10 cl oil / 100 g butter / 3 lemons / Parsley / Salt, pepper.

Prep: 15 min
Cooking: 15 min

Serves 4

Gut, wash and drain the trout. Season with salt and pepper. Roll them in the flour. Brown the chopped shallots in the oil and 30 g of butter in a fish pan.

Cook the trout in this hot mixture for 5 minutes on each side, spooning the cooking liquid over them regularly. When they are well cooked, arrange them on a serving dish.

Add the rest of the butter to the pan and let it heat until it is foamy.

Pour the foaming butter over the trout with the juice of 2 lemons. Sprinkle with chopped parsley.

Serve immediately.

THE WINE ROUTE

THE ALSATIAN WINE ROUTE IS A REMARKABLE ROUTE WHICH REVEALS NOT ONLY THE WEALTH OF THE ALSATIAN VINEYARDS BUT ALSO THE WONDERFUL, ATTRACTIVE LITTLE TOWNS, WITH THEIR CHARMING, ROMANTIC APPEARANCE.

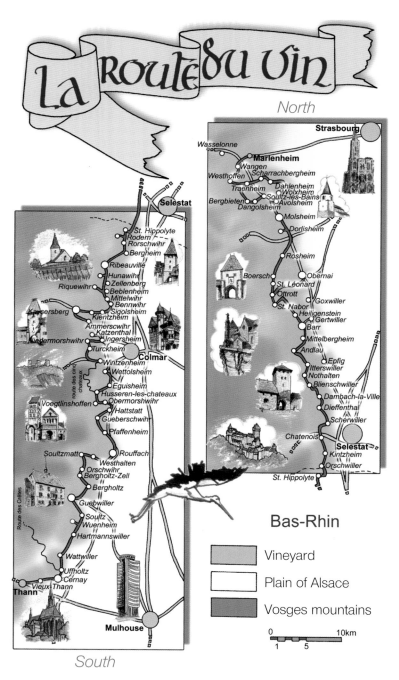

la route du vin

North

Strasbourg

Wasselonne
Marlenheim
Wangen
Westhoffen
Scharrachbergheim
Traenheim
Dahlenheim
Wolxheim
Bergbieten
Soultz-les-Bains
Dangolsheim
Avolsheim
Molsheim
Dorlisheim

Selestat

Rosheim

St. Hippolyte
Rodern
Rorschwihr
Bergheim

Boersch
Obernai
St. Léonard
Ottrott
St. Nabor
Goxwiller
Heiligenstein
Gertwiller
Barr

Ribeauvillé
Hunawihr
Zellenberg
Beblenheim
Mittelwihr
Bennwihr
Sigolsheim
Kientzheim

Riquewihr

Mittelbergheim
Andlau
Epfig
Itterswiller
Nothalten
Blienschwiller
Dambach-la-Ville
Dieffenthal
Scherwiller

Kaysersberg

Ammerschwihr
Katzenthal
Niedermorshwihr
Ingersheim
Turckheim

Colmar

Winzenheim
Wettolsheim

Eguisheim
Husseren-les-chateaux
Voegtlinshoffen
Obermorshwihr
Hattstatt
Gueberschwihr
Pfaffenheim

Chatenois
Selestat
Kintzheim
Orschwiller
St. Hippolyte

Soultzmatt
Rouffach
Westhalten
Orschwihr
Bergholtz-Zell
Bergholtz

Bas-Rhin

Guebwiller

Soultz
Wuenheim
Hartmannswiller

Wattwiller

Uffholtz
Cernay
Vieux-Thann
Thann

Mulhouse

route des cinq chateaux

Route des Crêtes

Vineyard

Plain of Alsace

Vosges mountains

0   10km
1 5

South

Haut-Rhin

Chicken with Riesling

1 chicken weighing about 1.500 kg / 50 g butter / 3 shallots / 1 clove of garlic / 5 cl cognac / 40 cl Riesling / 200 g button mushrooms / 20 cl fresh cream / Salt, pepper.

○**OOO** ✕✕   Prep: 10 min   Serves 6 ○
                    Cooking: 1 h

Chop the chicken into portion-sized pieces. Brown them in a casserole dish for 5 minutes, Season with salt and pepper. Keep warm.

Add the chopped shallots and garlic to the dish and flambée with cognac. Add the chicken. Deglaze with the Riesling. Add the button mushrooms. Check the seasoning. Leave to cook for 40 minutes on a gentle heat.

Remove the pieces of chicken and arrange them on a serving dish.

Reduce the cooking liquid and add the cream while stirring.

Pour the sauce over the chicken and serve immediately.

Alsatian chopped turkey

200 g of sauerkraut / 50 g butter / 1 kg chopped turkey / 25 cl fresh cream / 1 tin of button mushrooms / 1 stock cube / Croutons.

○○**OO** ✕   Prep: 15 min   Serves 6 ○
                    Cooking: 1 h 40 min

Wash the sauerkraut in cold water. Press it to extract the juice. Season with salt and pepper. Cook it in water for 1 hour 30 minutes.

Brown the chopped turkey in a saucepan with 30 g of butter. Remove the turkey and keep it to one side. Add the cream, mushrooms and crumbled stock cube to the gravy.

Pour in the drained sauerkraut and mix. Add the turkey to the pan to heat it. Mix. Turn out onto a plate.

Heat the rest of the butter in a frying pan. Cook the croutons and when they are golden, sprinkle them over the turkey mixture.

Pot-au-feu (Beef stew)

800 g beef rib / 800 g shoulder of beef / 2 leeks / 1/2 celery / 2 turnips / 4 carrots / 1 onion / 1 clove / 4 marrow bones / 6 large potatoes / 4 slices of bread / Mustard / Horseradish / Coarse salt / Salt and pepper.

Prep: 30 min
Cooking: 4 h

Serves 6

Place the meat, washed leeks, celery, peeled and diced turnips , peeled and sliced carrots, peeled onion spiked with cloves, and marrow bones into a large pan of boiling salted water. Season with salt and pepper.

Leave to simmer for 4 hours on a gentle heat and skim foam off the top at regular intervals.

Add the peeled potatoes 30 minutes before the end of cooking.

Arrange the meat and vegetables on a large hollow plate. Pour several ladles full of stock over them.

The marrow bone is eaten on bread seasoned with coarse salt.

Serve with mustard and horseradish.

Suggestion: it is traditional to serve the pot-au-feu with a selection of salad vegetables.

Liver Dumplings

400 g loin of pork / 200 g pig's liver / 100 g smoked bacon / 1 onion / 2 cloves of garlic / 2 eggs / 100 g of flour / Nutmeg / Parsley and chervil / Salt, pepper.

Prep: 20 min
Cooking: 10 min

Serves 4

Chop the pork loin, pig's liver, smoked bacon, onion and garlic very finely.

Put this mixture in a dish. Add the eggs, flour and nutmeg. Season with salt and pepper. Mix well. Season with parsley and chervil.

Boil 2 l of salted water.

Use two large spoons to shape the dumpling and place them gently in the boiling water. Leave to cook for ten minutes. The dumplings rise to the surface when they are cooked.

Drain them on a towel.

Suggestion: you can brown the cooked dumplings in hot butter. Serve with a green salad or sauerkraut.

Blade of smoked pork

1.5 l of stock / 2 carrots / 1 leek / 1 onion / 1/2 stalk of celery / 1 blade of smoked pork weighing 1.500 kg / Gherkins and pickled onions / Horseradish.

Prep: 15 min
Cooking: 1 h 30 min

Serves 6

Put the stock, carrots, leeks, onion and celery, peeled and chopped into small pieces in a large saucepan. Bring to the boil. Add the blade of smoked pork to this stock. Cook on a gentle heat for 1 hour 30 minutes.

Drain the blade and cut it into slices. Arrange these on a hollow plate. Place the gherkins and pickled onions around it. Serve with horseradish.

Smoked blade of pork is eaten with salad vegetables, sautéed potatoes or simply a green salad.

MEAT DISHES

Baker's stew – « Baeckeoffe »

500 g loin of pork (off the bone) / 500 g of shoulder of mutton (off the bone) / 500 g beef chuck (off the bone) / 4 carrots / 1 leek / 4 onions / 1 bouquet garni / 2 cloves / 75 cl white Alsatian wine / 30 g butter / 2 cloves of garlic / 1 kg potatoes / Salt, pepper.

○○●● ✗   Prep: 30 min – Cooking: 3 h   Serves 6
           Marinate: 24 h

Cut the meat into cubes. Put them into a casserole dish with the sliced carrots and leeks and the chopped onions. Add the bouquet garni and cloves. Season with salt and pepper. Pour the wine over the mixture and cover the dish with a cloth. Leave to marinate for 24 hours.

Butter a Baeckeoffe dish. Press the garlic around the edges of the dish.

Peel the potatoes and cut them into very fine slices. Cover the base of the dish with a layer of potato. Season with salt and pepper.

Place the meat on top. Add half the vegetables from the marinade. Fill up with the rest of the potatoes and vegetables. Season with salt and pepper. Pour the marinade over the mixture – the liquid should cover half the dish.

Hermetically seal the dish.

Cook in a gentle oven at 180° C (gas 6) for 3 hours.

This dish is served with a green salad and is eaten particularly in winter.

Sauerkraut

1.500 g of sauerkraut / 2 onions / 1 clove of garlic / 100 g of goose fat / 2 bay leaves / 2 cloves / 50 cl Sylvaner / 2 knuckles of ham / 2 smoked blades / 400 g smoked bacon / 6 large potatoes / 12 liver dumplings (p. 34) / 6 Strasbourg sausages / Salt, pepper.

Serves 6   Prep: 25 min
             Cooking: 3 h 15 min

Wash the sauerkraut in cold water. Drain it then wash it a second time. Press it to extract the water.

Brown the chopped onions and garlic in the goose fat heated in a casserole dish.

Add the sauerkraut. Season with salt and pepper.

Add the bay leaves and cloves.

Pour over the Sylvaner and water. Leave to cook for 1 hour on a medium heat.

Mix from time to time so that the fat is well distributed.

Add the knuckles of ham and smoked blade as well as the smoked bacon. Leave to simmer for 1 hour 30 minutes, making sure that there is always enough liquid.

Peel the potatoes. Put them on top of the sauerkraut and let it cook for another 20 minutes. During this time, poach the liver dumplings for 20 minutes and the Strasbourg sausages for 5 minutes.

Arrange the sauerkraut on a heated dish.

Garnish it with the meat, liver dumplings, Strasbourg sausages and potatoes.

Serve very hot.

Asparagus cakes

1 kg asparagus / 4 eggs / 10 cl fresh cream / 10 cl milk /
Nutmeg / 100 g flour / Salt, pepper.

Prep: 15 min – Cooking: 30 min   Serves 4
Rest time: 30 min

Peel and wash the asparagus. Cook it in salted water for
20 minutes.

Cut each stalk lengthways into 4 cm pieces.

In a bowl, mix the eggs, fresh cream and milk. Season
with salt and pepper and a little nutmeg. Fold the flour carefully into the batter. Leave to rest for 30 minutes.

Add the asparagus pieces to the batter.

Form small pancakes with a spoon and cook them in
an oiled pan, leaving to cook for 5 minutes on each side.

Red cabbage with apples

1 red cabbage / 1 sugar lump / 10 cl vinegar / 20 cl red wine / 100 g goose fat / 1 onion / 1 bay leaf / 3 cloves / 3 sweet apples / Salt, pepper.

Serves 6   Prep: 20 min – Cooking: 2 h
            Marinade: 30 min

Cut the cabbage into fine strips after removing the stalk. Wash the strips in cold water.

Put the cabbage and sugar lump in a dish. Season with salt and pepper. Pour over the vinegar and red wine. Leave to marinate for 30 minutes.

Melt the goose fat in a casserole dish. Add the chopped onion. Cover with the cabbage. Add the bay leaf and cloves. Pour over the vinegar and red wine. Cover and simmer on a moderate heat for 1 hour 30 minutes.

Peel the apples into fine strips. Arrange them on top of the cabbage. Leave to cook for a further 30 minutes.

Remove the bay leaf and cloves before serving.

Spätzle (Alsatian noodles)

200 g flour / 2 eggs / 25 g butter / 10 g salt.

○○○○● ✗   Prep: 15 min   Serves 4 ○
                 Cooking: 30 min

Mix the flour, eggs, 10 cl water and salt in a dish until you obtain a smooth dough.

Over a saucepan of boiling salted water, cut the dough into thin strips on a board and slide them into the water.

Leave to cook until the noodles rise to the surface (about 5 minutes).

Remove them with a slotted spoon.

Turn them in hot butter, making sure they do not burn.

Smoked potatoes

200 g butter / 2 kg potatoes / 3 onions / 150 g smoked bacon cubes / Salt, pepper.

○○○○● ✗   Prep: 10 min   Serves 8 ○
                 Cooking: 1 h 20 min

Butter a cast iron casserole dish generously.

Peel, wash and slice the potatoes.

Place a layer of potatoes at the bottom, then a layer of chopped onions. Season with salt and pepper.

Blanch the bacon cubes and put them on top. Cover with the remaining potatoes. Season with salt and pepper. Dot with knobs of butter.

Put the lid on the dish and cook in a very hot oven for 1 hour 20 minutes at 220° C (gas 7-8).

Potato cakes

1 kg of large potatoes / 2 eggs / 2 onions / Chives and parsley / 20 g butter / Salt, pepper.

Serves 6   Prep: 15 min
              Cooking: 10 min

Peel the potatoes. Grate them. Leave them to drain in a colander.

In a bowl, mix the potato with the eggs and chopped onions. Season with salt and pepper. Add the chives and parsley.

Mix well to obtain a paste.

Heat the butter in a frying pan.

Use two spoons to form round cakes which you put in the pan.

Fry them for 5 minutes on each side.

Serve immediately with a green salad.

Carnival fritters

500 g flour / 100 g granulated sugar / 2 eggs / 1 teaspoon oil / 25 cl milk / 10 g brewer's yeast / 20 g icing sugar / Powdered cinnamon / A pinch of salt.

Prep: 15 min – Cooking: 10 min   Serves 6
Resting time: 1 h

Sieve the flour into a bowl. Make a hollow and put the sugar, eggs, oil, milk, salt and brewer's yeast into it. Knead this mixture quickly to obtain a smooth, supple dough. Leave to rest for 1 hour.

Roll out the dough to 1 cm thick on a floured board.

Cut out lozenges, 4 cm per side.

Fry in a fish-fryer. The fritters are ready when they rise to the surface.

Drain them and serve sprinkled with icing sugar and cinnamon.

Apple fritters

4 eggs / 2 egg whites / 350 g flour / 4 dl of oil / 6 apples / 20 g of granulated sugar / a pinch of salt.

Prep: 15 min – Cooking: 10 min   Serves 6
Resting time: 1 h

Beat the 4 whole eggs and salt as if for an omelette. Add the flour gradually.

Stir while adding 4 dl of water until you obtain a smooth batter. Leave to rest for 1 hour.

Beat the 2 egg-whites to a firm snow and fold them carefully into the batter along with the oil.

Peel the apples. Remove the cores while keeping the apples whole. Slice them into rings.

Dip the apple rings in the batter and then fry them for 6 to 8 minutes.

Drain the fritters. Sprinkle sugar over them.

Kougelhopf

25 g brewer's yeast / 30 cl milk / 200 g butter / 80 g granulated sugar / 500 g flour / 2 eggs / 100 g raisins / 150 g whole almonds / A pinch of salt.

◯◯**OO** ✗✗   Prep: 1 h – Cooking: 45 min   Serves 6 to 8
Proving time: 2 h

Mix the yeast with 15 cl of heated milk.

Mix the butter, sugar and salt into the remaining 15 cl of milk.

Put the flour and eggs into a bowl and add the butter-sugar-salt mixture. Mix vigorously, beating the dough for 20 minutes, lifting it with your hands and beating it against the walls of the bowl. The dough must not stick to your hands when it is ready. Then add the yeast-milk mixture. Cover the bowl and leave the dough to prove for 1 hour in a warm place.

Soak the raisins in a little luke-warm water to make them swell, then fold them carefully into the dough.

Butter a kougelhopf mould. Arrange the almonds at the bottom of the mould.

Put the dough into the mould. Place the mould in a warm place and leave to prove again. It should slightly overlap the edge of the mould.

Bake in the oven at 150° C (gas 5) for 45 minutes.

Halfway through the baking time, cover with aluminium foil to prevent it from becoming too brown.

Smooth cottage cheese with strawberries

500 g strawberries / 1 kg smooth cottage cheese / 25 cl fresh cream / 1 egg / 50 g granulated sugar.

 Prep: 15 min   Serves 8
Resting: 1 h

Wash the strawberries and remove the stalks. Crush them with a fork.

Mix the smooth cottage cheese with the fresh cream. Add the egg yolk and sugar.

Beat the egg-white into a firm snow and fold it carefully into the mixture.

Add the crushed strawberries.

Put into the fridge for 1 hour.

Mendiant

5 stale milk rolls / 50 cl boiling milk / 1 packet (2 tea-spoons) vanilla sugar / 100 g granulated sugar / 4 eggs / the zest of 1 lemon / Powdered cinnamon / 2 cl kirsch / 400 g stoned black cherries / 400 g apples / 50 g butter.

Prep: 20 min   Serves 6
Cooking: 1 h

Grate the crusts of the rolls and reserve the crumbs.

Bring the milk to a boil with the vanilla sugar.

Pour this mixture over the rolls to soak them. Crush them with a balloon whisk.

Add the sugar, egg yolks, lemon zest, cinnamon and kirsch. Mix with the cherries and sliced apples. Beat the egg whites to a firm snow and fold them into the preparation.

Butter a cake mould generously. Pour the mixture into the mould, sprinkle with the grated crumbs and dot with knobs of butter.

Bake in a hot oven at 220° C (gas 7-8) for 1 hour.

Mendiant, also known as «bettelmann» can be served luke-warm or cold.

DESSERTS

Fruit cake
« Bereweche »

50 g hazelnuts / 50 g almonds / 50 g walnuts / 100 g prunes / 100 g dried pears / 100 g dried figs / 100 g dried bananas / 100 g dried apples / 50 g raisins / 1 lemon / 10 cl kirsch / 5 g powdered cinnamon / 200 g bread dough.

Serves 8   Prep: 20 min
             Cooking: 35 min

✗ OOO ○

Chop the hazelnuts, almonds and walnuts.

Cut the prunes, pears, figs, bananas and apples into long pieces. Mix everything with the raisins.

Add the lemon juice and kirsch. Add the cinnamon. Mix this into the bread dough. When it is evenly mixed, shape it into an oval loaf.

Bake in the oven at 220° C (gas 7-8) for 35 minutes.

Streusel

For the dough: *25 g brewer's yeast / 20 cl milk / 275 g flour / 125 g butter / 30 g granulated sugar / 125 g butter / 100 g flour / 1 teaspoon of powdered cinnamon / 50 g of granulated sugar / Icing sugar.*

○○**OO** ✕✕   Prep: 20 min – Cooking: 30 min   Serves 6 ◯
             Proving time: 1 h

Mix the yeast and the luke-warm milk.

Mix the flour, softened butter and sugar. Add the yeast and knead together.

Roll out the dough to about 3 cm thick.

Butter a mould and put the dough in it.

Prepare the «streusel» mixture. Melt the butter. Add the flour, granulating sugar and cinnamon. Mix and leave to cool.

Spoon the streusel on top of the dough.

Leave the cake to prove in a luke-warm place for 1 hour.

Bake in a hot oven at 180° C (gas 6) for 30 minutes.

Sprinkle with cinnamon and icing sugar.

Bilberry tart

150 g flour / 75 g butter / 1 kg bilberries / 30 g granulated sugar / A pinch of salt.

○○○**O** ✕   Prep: 10 min – Cooking: 35 min   Serves 8 ◯
            Resting time: 1 h

Mix the flour and salt. Add the softened butter.

Rub it between your fingers until it has the consistency of breadcrumbs. Add 10 cl of water. Form into a ball. Leave to rest for 1 hour.

Roll out the pastry. Use it to line a buttered tart tin.

Add the bilberries. Sprinkle with sugar. Bake in a hot oven at 210° C (gas 7) for 35 minutes.

Cheesecake

150 g flour / 75 g butter.
300 g smooth cottage cheese / 4 eggs / 125 g granulated
sugar / Vanilla sugar / 5 cl milk / 25 cl thick fresh cream /
50 g cornstarch / 50 g raisins / 25 g flour / Icing sugar / A
pinch of salt.

○○○● ✗✗   Prep: 20 min – Cooking: 35 min   Serves 6
             Resting time: 1 h

Mix the flour and salt. Add the softened butter and rub it between your fingers until it resembles breadcrumbs. Add 10 cl water. Form a ball. Leave to rest for 1 hour.

Line a buttered tart tin with this pastry. Prick the base and shape fairly high edges.

Mix the smooth cottage cheese, egg yolks, sugar, vanilla sugar, milk, cream, cornstarch and raisins. Fold in the flour. Beat the egg-whites into a firm snow and fold them into the mixture. When the mixture is smooth, spoon it onto the pastry.

Bake in a hot oven at 220° C (gas 7-8) for 35 minutes.

When the tart is baked, turn it out carefully onto a grid. Leave to cool.

Turn it over back into its original position. Sprinkle with icing sugar.

You can soak the raisins in a little rum.

Apple tart

150 g flour / 75 g butter / 1 kg apples / 10 cl liquid fresh cream / 10 cl milk / 2 eggs / 100 g granulated sugar / A pinch of salt.

○○**OO** ✗✗   Prep: 15 min – Cooking: 30 min   Serves 6   ◡
                Resting time: 1 h

    Mix the flour and salt. Add the softened butter and rub it between your fingers until it resembles breadcrumbs. Add 10 cl water. Form a ball. Leave to rest for 1 hour.

    Roll out the pastry and line a tart tin with it.

    Peel the apples. Cut into quarters. Arrange them in the tin.

    Bake in a hot oven at 240° C (gas 8) for 10 minutes.

    Beat the liquid cream, milk, eggs and sugar. Pour this mixture into the tart tin.

    Continue baking for a further 20 minutes at 180° C (gas 6). Serve luke-warm.

Quetsch plum tart

For the pastry: *250 g flour / 10 g yeast / 50 g granulated sugar / 125 g butter / 2 eggs / 10 cl milk / 1 kg quetsch plums / 100 g granulated sugar / Powdered cinnamon.*

○○○**O** ✗✗   Prep: 20 min – Cooking: 35 min   Serves 6   ◡
                Resting time: 2 h

    Mix the flour, yeast, sugar and softened butter in a bowl. Add the eggs one by one while mixing. Bind with the milk. Leave the dough to prove for 2 hours in the refrigerator.

    Stone the quetsch plums.

    Roll out the dough and use it to line a buttered tart tin.

    Arrange the quetsch plums in the tin. Sprinkle with granulated sugar.

    Bake in a hot oven at 200° C (gas 6-7) for 35 minutes.

    Sprinkle a little cinnamon over it just before serving.

Little aniseed biscuits

3 eggs / 400 g granulated sugar / 3 lemons / 400 g flour / 20 g butter / 2 tablespoons of aniseed.

Prep: 20 min – Cooking: 10 min   Serves 8
Resting time: 1 h + 24 h

Separate the egg whites from the yolks.

Mix the sugar with the whites. Add the yolks and zest of 3 lemons. Mix well. Add the lemon juice. Fold the flour into the mixture while continuing to stir well.

Leave to rest for 1 hour.

Spoon onto a buttered oven tray and sprinkle with aniseed.

Leave to dry overnight. Bake at 180° C (gas 6) until they are golden.

Little Christmas biscuits

500 g flour / 250 g granulated sugar / 250 g butter / 9 egg yolks / 10 cl milk.

Prep: 15 min – Cooking: 10 min   Serves 8
Resting time: 2 h

Mix the flour, sugar, butter and 8 egg yolks. Leave to rest for 2 hours.

Butter an oven tray. Roll out the pastry. Cut out into different shapes, hearts, stars, etc. Lay them on the oven tray.

Mix the last egg yolk with the milk and brush over the biscuits.

Bake in a hot oven at 220° C (gas 7-8) for 10 minutes.

INDEX OF RECIPES

Soups

Riewele soup	4
Lentil soup	4
Onion soup with melted cheese	5

Cold hors d'œuvres

Alsatian asparagus	6
Dandelion salad	8
Potato salad	8
Alsatian salad	9
Foie gras	10
Smooth cottage cheese/ quark with fresh cream	12
Savoury kougelhopf	12

Hot hors d'œuvres

Filled Cervelat	14
Stuffed potatoes	14
Alsatian snails	16
Breaded Munster cheese	18
Gnocchi	18
«Tartes flambées»	20
Onion tart	20
Valley Pie	22

Fish dishes

Fried carp	24
Sauerkraut with fish	24
Trout with almonds	26
Trout Meunière	26

Meat dishes

Chicken with Riesling	30
Alsatian chopped turkey	30
Pot-au-feu	32
Liver Dumplings	34
Blade of smoked pork	34
Baker's stew – «Baeckeoffe»	36
Sauerkraut	37

Side dishes

Asparagus cakes	40
Red cabbage with apples	41
Spätzle (Alsatian noodles)	42
Smoked potatoes	42
Potato cakes	43

Desserts

Carnival fritters	44
Apple fritters	44
Kougelhopf	46
Smooth cottage cheese with strawberries	48
Mendiant	48
Fruit cake «Bereweche»	49
Streusel	50
Bilberry tart	50
Cheesecake	52
Apple tart	54
Quetsch plum tart	54
Little aniseed biscuits	56
Little Christmas biscuits	56

© Dormonval, 2006

Dépôt légal 2ᵉ trim. 2006 n° 3 163

Imprimé en U.E.